W9-AKD-118

PAPL
DISCARDED

JOHN M CUELENAERE PUBLIC LIBRARY

LEAVING MY HOMELAND

After the Journey

My New Home After Iraq

CRABTREE
PUBLISHING COMPANY
WWW.CRABTREEBOOKS.COM

Ellen Rodger

CRABTREE
PUBLISHING COMPANY
WWW.CRABTREEBOOKS.COM

Author: Ellen Rodger

Editors: Sarah Eason, Harriet McGregor, and Janine Deschenes

Proofreader and indexer: Wendy Scavuzzo

Editorial director: Kathy Middleton

Design: Paul Myerscough and Jessica Moon

Cover design: Samara Parent

Photo research: Rachel Blount

Production coordinator and
    Prepress technician: Ken Wright

Print coordinator: Katherine Berti

Consultants: Hawa Sabriye and HaEun Kim, Centre for Refugee Studies,
    York University

Produced for Crabtree Publishing Company by Calcium Creative

Publisher's Note: The story presented in this book is a fictional account
based on extensive research of real-life accounts by refugees, with the aim
of reflecting the true experience of refugee children and their families.

Photo Credits:
t=Top, c=Center, b=Bottom, l= Left, r=Right

Inside: Shutterstock: Annasunny24: p. 15br; Best-Backgrounds: p. 9t;
Creative Stall: pp. 12bl, 12bc; Dboystudio: p. 25t; Elenabsl: p. 14br; ESB
Professional: p. 12c; Feelplus: pp. 18t, 19tr; Lena Ha: p. 7; Jasminko
Ibrakovic: p. 15l; Isovector: p. 15tr; Jemastock: p. 11r; Lawkeeper: p. 23t;
Cindy Lee: p. 4r; LineTale: p. 28b; Loveshop: p. 4l; James R. Martin:
pp. 14-15t; Minto.ong: p. 17bl; Enzo Molinari: p. 17br; Monkey Business
Images: pp. 12-13b; Ruud Morijn Photographer: p. 29c; Mspoint:
p. 28t; Nagel Photography: pp. 21, 22-23; Angela Ostafichuk: p. 8; Karen
Roach: p. 18c; Rvector: p. 25b; Dina Saeed: p. 20l; Kate Scott: p. 9; Serkan
Senturk: pp. 5, 6; John T Takai: p. 26t; Tashal: p. 16; What's My Name:
p. 10b; Juriaan Wossink: p. 10; Murat Irfan Yalcin: p. 3; Zurijeta:
pp. 20r, 24, 27; UNHCR: © UNHCR/Evelyn Hockstein: p. 11t; ©
UNHCR/Betty Press: p. 17t; © UNHCR/Sebastian Rich: pp. 11b, 19t;
Visual Hunt: Knight Foundation on Visualhunt/CC BY-SA: p. 26b;
Lion Multimedia Production USA: pp. 22b, 23b.

Cover: © UNHCR/Sebastian Rich

Library and Archives Canada Cataloguing in Publication

Rodger, Ellen, author
    My new home after Iraq / Ellen Rodger.

(Leaving my homeland : after the journey)
Includes index.
Issued in print and electronic formats.
ISBN 978-0-7787-4975-2 (hardcover).--
ISBN 978-0-7787-4988-2 (softcover).--ISBN 978-1-4271-2124-0 (HTML)

    1. Refugees--Iraq--Juvenile literature. 2. Refugees--United States--
Juvenile literature. 3. Refugee children--Iraq--Juvenile literature.
4. Refugee children--United States--Juvenile literature. 5. Refugees--
United States--Social conditions--Juvenile literature. 6. Refugees--Social
conditions--Juvenile literature. 7. Iraq--Social conditions--Juvenile
literature. I. Title.

HV640.5.I76R633 2018   j305.9'06914095670973   C2018-903012-7
    C2018-903013-5

Library of Congress Cataloging-in-Publication Data

Names: Rodger, Ellen, author.
Title: My new home after Iraq / Ellen Rodger.
Description: New York : Crabtree Publishing, [2019] |
  Series: Leaving my homeland: after the journey | Includes index.
Identifiers: LCCN 2018029235 (print) | LCCN 2018032290 (ebook) |
  ISBN 9781427121240 (Electronic) |
  ISBN 9780778749752 (hardcover) |
  ISBN 9780778749882 (pbk.)
Subjects: LCSH: Refugees--Iraq--Juvenile literature. | Refugees--Michigan-
  -Juvenile literature. | Refugee children--Michigan--Juvenile literature. |
  Iraqis--Michigan--Juvenile literature.
Classification: LCC HV640.5.I76 (ebook) |
  LCC HV640.5.I76 R629 2019 (print) | DDC 956.7044/31--dc23
LC record available at https://lccn.loc.gov/2018029235

Crabtree Publishing Company
www.crabtreebooks.com   1-800-387-7650

Printed in the U.S.A./092018/CG20180719

Copyright © **2019 CRABTREE PUBLISHING COMPANY.** All rights reserved. No part of this publication may be reproduced, stored in a retrieval
system or be transmitted in any form or by any means, electronic, mechanical, photocopying, recording, or otherwise, without the prior written
permission of Crabtree Publishing Company. In Canada: We acknowledge the financial support of the Government of Canada through the
Canada Book Fund for our publishing activities.

Published in Canada
Crabtree Publishing
616 Welland Ave.
St. Catharines, Ontario
L2M 5V6

Published in the United States
Crabtree Publishing
PMB 59051
350 Fifth Avenue, 59th Floor
New York, New York 10118

Published in the United Kingdom
Crabtree Publishing
Maritime House
Basin Road North, Hove
BN41 1WR

Published in Australia
Crabtree Publishing
3 Charles Street
Coburg North
VIC, 3058

What Is in This Book?

Zainab's Story: Iraq to the United States

As-salaam 'alaykum! (Peace be with you!) *Hello! My name is Zainab, and I live in Dearborn, Michigan, in the United States. I came here with Abbi (my father), Ummi (my mother), and my older sisters Aisha and Mariam. Iraq is the country where I was born. I lived in a city called Ramadi. It is where my grandmother, uncles, aunts, and cousins still live. I was a* **refugee**.

The US flag

The writing on the Iraqi flag is called the Takbir. It means God is the greatest.

UN Rights of the Child

A child's family has the **responsibility** to help ensure their **rights** are protected and to help them learn to exercise their rights. Think about these rights as you read this book.

My family left Iraq because of the Iraq War. The war started in 2003, the year I was born. It ended in 2011, but there is still fighting and **terrorism**. *People are killed every day. During the war, Abbi worked as a translator for an American company. Because of this, his life was in danger. That is why we fled Iraq.*

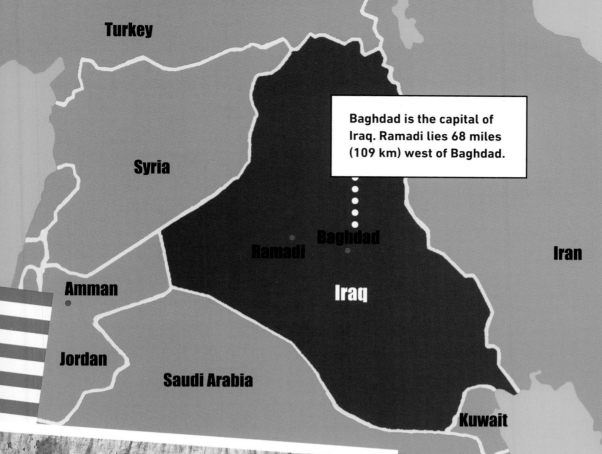

Turkey

Syria

Baghdad is the capital of Iraq. Ramadi lies 68 miles (109 km) west of Baghdad.

Baghdad

Ramadi

Iran

Iraq

Amman

Jordan

Saudi Arabia

Kuwait

The war in Iraq was mainly fought between Iraq and the United States. The fighting has damaged much of the country. There is still no peace in Iraq.

At first, we went to the city of Amman in Jordan. But life was hard. Refugees are not allowed to work there. My family could not make the money we needed to survive. But we were lucky because we were eventually told that we could go to live in the United States. We were so happy!

My Homeland, Iraq

Iraq has a lot of desert, but it also has two of the world's best-known rivers: the Tigris and the Euphrates. The rivers made the land around them good for farming. Many ancient **cultures** developed in this area, including the Sumerians. They invented the wheel and the earliest forms of writing.

Farming is still important in Iraq today, but the country's biggest industry is oil. Money made from oil sales is helping Iraq recover from years of war and fighting. However, things are still not settled. **Extremist** groups such as the **Islamic State in Iraq and the Levant (ISIL)** have taken over some areas of the country. The Iraqi Army and other groups are fighting to free these areas.

It is thought that it will cost $88 billion to rebuild Iraq. There is much that needs to be done, including rebuilding roads, cities, homes, hospitals, and schools.

Police officers guard the streets in cities such as Mosul, where ISIL has been very powerful.

The war and conflict, or fighting, has torn families apart. Violence has forced many Iraqi people to flee their homes and settle in other parts of Iraq. They are known as **internally displaced persons (IDPs)**. Some Iraqis were held by ISIL as prisoners in their own homes and cities. Some left to go to nearby countries as refugees.

For Iraqis living abroad, it is difficult to watch, hear, and read about the violence in their homeland. They worry about the safety of the family and friends they left behind.

Story in Numbers

More than

2.9 million

Iraqis are IDPs.

More than

1.4 million

Iraqis live in **temporary** homes.

7

Zainab's Story: Leaving My Homeland

I had never been on an airplane before we came to the United States. It was very exciting and scary. I felt like a bird flying away to freedom! In Amman, we had safety, but Abbi could not work and it could not be our home.

We did not bring a lot with us to the United States. Before we lived in Jordan, we had already left everything behind in Iraq. We could not go back to say goodbye to our family in Iraq. This made Ummi very sad. She said coming to the United States was for us children. It was to save our lives and to give us a home in which we could be safe.

Women and girls often have more opportunities and freedoms in the United States than they do in Iraq.

Story in Numbers

There are an estimated

1.5 million

Iraqi refugees in Jordan, Turkey, Syria, Lebanon, and Egypt. Most of them are not **registered**.

United States
Detroit

Amman
Jordan

The journey from Amman, Jordan, to Detroit is more than 6,000 miles (9,656 km).

At the airport in Detroit, we met my father's cousin, Humam. He has lived in Detroit for many years. He said people call him Hugh, because his Iraqi name confuses Americans. They say "your name, it sounds like 'human' or 'who man'!" I like the name Humam, though, because it is the name of a famous soccer player in Iraq. And I love soccer!

Refugees may feel relieved when their airplane lands in their new country. However, they can also feel unsettled by the new culture they find there.

At the airport, Humam was with an American man. His name was Steve. Abbi told me that Steve worked with a place that helps refugees.

A New Life

Refugees face being treated badly, violence, and even death in their homelands. Many are desperate to leave, but it is not easy for them to find a new home in another country. Less than 1 percent of the world's refugees are **resettled** permanently in safe countries. Most refugees find temporary homes in the countries that border, or are next to, their homeland. Some live for years in places where they cannot become citizens.

The **United Nations High Commissioner for Refugees (UNHCR)** provides protection and assistance for refugees all over the world. The UNHCR registers refugees who are then passed on to countries that take in refugees.

The UNHCR provides health care, clothes, and shelter to people who have fled their homes.

Story in Numbers

To be accepted in the United States, a refugee must undergo at least:
5 background checks
4 security checks
3 in-person interviews
2 other **agency** security checks

The UNHCR and other groups help refugees with tasks such as filling out forms.

Iraqi refugees celebrate their freedom in their new home in Louisville, Kentucky.

Iraqi **asylum**-seekers who are chosen for resettlement go through a checking process. This takes years and is very difficult. The country accepting the refugees wants to make sure the refugees have not carried out serious crimes. Refugees are interviewed and checked many times. The UNHCR does the first **screenings**. The country accepting the refugees then interviews them again.

Zainab's Story: Arriving in Michigan

I do not remember a lot about my first night in the United States, but I do remember that I was very tired. We stayed with Humam's family. His wife Leyla prepared a big meal, and later, I slept in a big bed with my sisters. It felt good to have cousins in our new country and our new city of Dearborn.

Dearborn is called the **Arab** capital of North America, because so many Arabs like me live here. There are Arab bakeries, food stores, and also Arab lawyers and doctors. Leyla took us to some stores to buy new clothes. She owns a beauty salon. We went there and I got my hair cut!

Many Muslim girls and women wear hijab, a Muslim head covering.

We stayed with Humam's family for a week. Steve from the agency found us an apartment. He also helped us register for school. I have to share a bedroom with my sisters. That is okay. If I get scared at night, Aisha and Mariam are there. However, Ummi is still very sad. Abbi bought a phone for her, so she can talk to our family in Iraq. I like the phone, too, because Ummi let me text my cousins in Ramadi, back in Iraq!

Story in Numbers

5.6 million
Iraqis are refugees.

2.6 million
Iraqis are IDPs.

262,758
Iraqi refugees live in countries that border Iraq.

Many schools in Dearborn provide extra lessons for children who need help learning to read, write, and speak Englsh.

Hello from Dearborn!
We are all well. I hope you are well, too. This week, a woman from a place called the International Institution took us to a market. It was unbelievable. So much food with so many shelves of cereal! I will tell you a secret: Cereal is my favorite American food. But Ummi thinks it is yucky! I will tell you more about the United States and my new school soon, okay? Ma'a as-salaama Ila-liqaa (Goodbye until we meet again) Zainab

A New Home

For refugees, moving to a new country can be frightening. Everything is new, from the language to the money that people use. It takes time to **adjust**. In the United States, the government and groups called resettlement agencies help refugees when they first arrive. These groups want refugees to understand the American way of life.

When a refugee arrives, workers from the resettlement agency meet them at the airport. The workers help refugees find homes, schools, and doctors. They help them apply to work in the United States. When a refugee has a job, they pay **taxes** to the government. Refugees also repay the government the cost of their airfare to the United States.

This market in Dearborn sells food that is familiar to Arab **immigrants** and refugees.

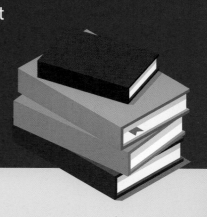

UN Rights of the Child

Children have the right to information from newspapers, books, computers, and other sources that affect their well-being.

Refugees receive money for their first 90 days in the country. However, they are not given a lot of money and they have to spend it carefully. Food and rent, or payment for somewhere to live, can be expensive. Sometimes refugees go to food banks or use food stamps to eat. Food banks are places that give out free food to people in need. Food stamps are vouchers that can be exchanged for food. They may also be given old furniture to help them set up their homes.

Refugees may be treated by doctors from their homeland to help them feel more comfortable and put them at ease.

Zainab's Story: My New Home

I love the Fourth of July fireworks here. But, the first time I heard them, I was very scared. I thought it was gunfire in the park near our new apartment. I even ran to hide. I was afraid the war had started here, too. Ummi and my sisters forgot that I had never heard fireworks before. When we left Iraq, there were no fireworks. Just bombs, gunshots, and fires.

Our apartment is nice. The electricity does not shut off at all like it did in Iraq. I can put pictures on the wall in my room. But not in Aisha's space. Aisha is very grumpy. She has a hard time learning English. Each week, she goes to classes with Ummi. Mariam and I go to school together.

Story in Numbers

84,902

Iraqis were allowed into the United States from 2007 to 2013 under the US Refugee Admissions Program (USRAP).

16

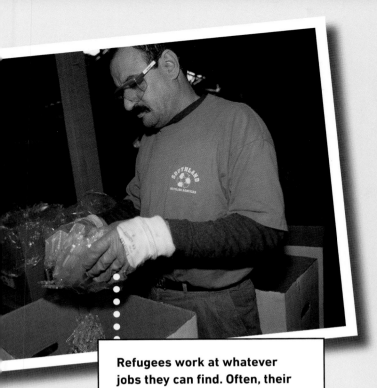

Refugees work at whatever jobs they can find. Often, their education and training from their home country is not accepted in their new country.

Good news! Abbi has a job. It is not a job like he had in Iraq. But it is much better than in Jordan. He says, "It is a start." Soon he will go back to school to train for another job. Abbi also gives us "real life" English lessons each day. Sometimes, we cook an American dinner from a recipe. One time, Mariam chose macaroni and cheese. Ummi was happy that we had cooked, but I do not think she liked the food! She kept wrinkling her nose.

One other school project we have is a making a movie. We use Abbi's phone to take videos. Aisha and Mariam plan them out. I am the "actress!" They are just little movies. We send them to family and friends back home in Iraq.

Trying out new foods can be fun—and sending photos of them to friends and family shows what life is like for refugees in their new countries.

17

A New School

When refugees are resettled in a safe country, their lives are no longer in danger. However, this does not mean that they live without fear. Living in a new country with a new language and culture is not easy.

Resettlement countries offer classes in language and culture. These classes help refugees learn things that most citizens of the country already know. These things may include using money or filling out forms in English. It is not that refugees are not smart, it is just that things are done differently in their home countries.

Government resettlement agencies sometimes direct refugees to other organizations that can help them. Samaritas is a church organization that is also a resettlement agency. It helps refugee famillies understand the school system, and helps schools understand refugees better.

I PLEDGE A
TO THE FLA
UNITED STAT
AND TO THE REPUBLIC FOR WHICH
ONE NATION UNDER GOD, INDIVISI
WITH LIBERTY AND JUSTICE FOR A

Refugee children learn the pledge of allegiance in American schools.

UN Rights of the Child

Children have the right to an education that helps develop their talents, skills, and abilities.

This teacher is helping a refugee student learn about the American flag.

One thing all refugees must do is start over. For adults, this can mean going back to school to get American qualifications to work in certain jobs. Even if they were teachers or dentists in their homeland, they will not be hired for those jobs in the United States unless they have American qualifications.

Learning to speak the language can be especially tough. It is often easier for children than adults. Refugees learn the language in school, on the playground, and from television shows, music, or the Internet. They also make friends with other children who speak only English. Some schools have programs especially for kids who do not speak English.

$ $ $

Zainab's Story: A New Way of Learning

Today, we got our report cards. My teacher says my English is very good. This is because I work so hard. It has been a challenge for me. Things make sense in my head. Then, when I write in English, it comes out too long. I have to go back and write it again. Sometimes I lose my Arabic words, too! Ummi asks me a question in Arabic, and I answer in English. I send emails to my cousin Qusay in Iraq. Sometimes I write them in Arabic, so I do not forget my language.

Some children read bilingual books. These books have a story in both Arabic and English. This helps them to learn the language.

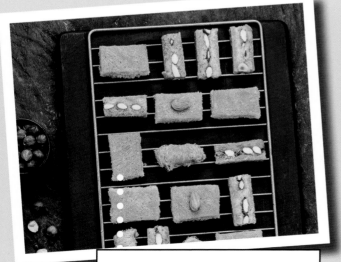

Kunafa is a favorite Middle Eastern treat made with sweet cheese wrapped in pastry.

Mariam is also a good student. She goes to high school now. Aisha takes classes for adults at night. Abbi is also taking night classes. He is training to be an **accountant**. During the day, Aisha and Ummi work at a bakery. It is an Arab bakery that makes delicious treats. People come from all over to buy their pita and kunafa (dessert).

Story in Numbers

The UN says there are

8.7 million

people in Iraq that need assistance, such as food, shelter, health care, and protection.

Dear Qusay,

We are all well (except Ummi, who misses everyone so much). I am happy to tell you that I went on a trip this week! At school, my class visited the Detroit Institute of Arts. It is a museum. Qusay, they have ancient Iraqi art there! We saw a lot of ancient pieces of art, including some from Nimrud. Abbi says that is a city near Mosul, in the north of Iraq. I felt proud of my homeland. It seems funny that I am learning about Iraq here in the United States! How is everything with you? Please give my love to all.

Ma'a as-salaama Ila-liqaa

(Goodbye until we meet again)

Zainab

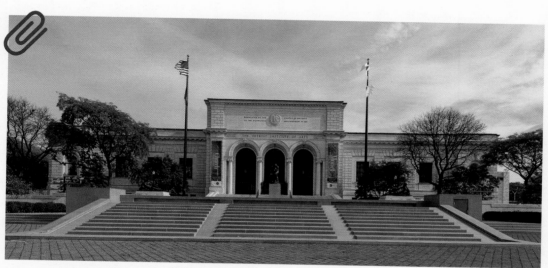

I loved visiting the Detroit Institute of Arts!

Everything Changes

Iraqi refugees come from a war-torn country. Those who arrived in the United States after the Iraq War are people who helped the US military or US companies in Iraq. They are the lucky ones. The US government understood that their lives were in danger because of the work they did, and offered them asylum.

The Islamic Center of America is a **mosque** and community center in Dearborn. It is the largest mosque in North America. It serves people from 62 different nationalities who belong to the Shia branch of Islam.

Refugee children can share their stories in places such as the Islamic Center.

Children have the right to follow and practice their own culture, language, and religion.

In the United States, resettlement agencies help refugees make a new start. Refugees also rely on mosques for help, because many Iraqi refugees feel more comfortable with people who speak their language and follow their religion.

The Refugee Assistance Program (RAP) is a government program that works with many agencies to help refugees resettle. These include Samaritas and the International Institute of Metropolitan Detroit. There are also many other smaller groups that help refugees in individual communities.

Meeting with other refugees helps women share advice and support each other while trying to settle in a new country.

Zainab's Story: My New Way of Life

For two years, I have been playing on the girls' soccer team at school. There are many girls like me who wear a hijab while they play. We use a special sports hijab with Velcro and magnets that make it safe if pulled. I love soccer so much. I could have never played on a team like this in Iraq. Abbi says I can play in a city league this summer. But I must keep my grades up.

Ummi's friend from the bakery says I am lucky. They live in another part of the United States. Her daughter was ordered to remove her hijab to play soccer. When the girl said no, she was told to leave the game. That makes me angry.

Sports are a wonderful way to bring people of all backgrounds together.

My sisters and I have started taking pictures of our life in Dearborn. We share them with family in Iraq. Mariam even has an Instagram account! She takes pictures and shares stories in Arabic and English. They make our grandmother in Iraq feel better when she is lonely for us. Last year at her high school, Mariam learned how to make films. She made one about Ummi learning American ways and her fear that we would lose our values and culture in the United States. It made me see how hard Ummi works and how important we are to her.

Posting photographs and messages on social media allows people to share their stories in their own perspective.

UN Rights of the Child

You have the right to freedom of expression in talking, writing, art, or through any media of your choice.

Zainab's Story: Looking to the Future

Today, we celebrated Eid Al-adha. This is one of our most important Muslim festivals! Ummi bought us new clothes. I gave Mariam and Aisha cards that I painted at school. We went to the mosque. I saw my friends Fatima and Madina from school there. Later, we went to Humam and Leyla's home for a big feast. Leyla made brownies. She knows it is an American treat that I love.

I am getting used to the United States. It is feeling like home now. My school has an all-nations day every year, when we learn about different countries. This year, I gave a speech on coming to the United States as a refugee. Abbi took me to the Arab American National Museum right here in Dearborn. I learned that Arab Americans have lived here for more than 140 years.

UN Rights of the Child

You have the right to live in a safe environment with hopes and dreams for the future.

The Arab American National Museum in Dearborn celebrates Arab-American history and culture.

Soon we can become American citizens. There will be a ceremony and celebrations after. I wish my family in Iraq could be here to see it. They left Ramadi because ISIL terrorists were fighting with the government troops. Now they live in Baghdad. Things are very difficult for them.

Someday, when it is safe, I hope to visit Iraq. I want to see my family again. I will show them pictures of my new country, the United States.

Eid celebrations always include lots of delicious foods.

Dear Qusay,
Eid Saeed (Happy Eid)! I have so much to tell you. We have lived in the United States for five years now. I am studying hard. I want to be a teacher someday, or maybe an engineer (a person who often works with or designs technology and machinery).
Aisha has a new job! She works for three days a week at cousin Leyla's salon. She is not so grouchy now! This makes Ummi happy. Abbi is happy, too. He has to complete just a few more courses. Then he will be an American accountant. He gave me a soccer ball and a kitten for an Eid gift. I have named the kitten "Bey," because she is beautiful, like my favorite singer.
Kul'am wa enta bi-khair
(May every year find you in good health)
Zainab

27

Do Not Forget Our Stories!

It takes about five years before a refugee can become a US citizen. In those years, the refugee must find work to support him or herself. Not everyone is friendly to refugees. Sometimes, refugees experience **racism** or hatred of their religion. Many organizations help to teach refugees about the American way of life. They also help make sure their rights are respected.

Refugees contribute, or give something, to the economy and culture of the countries in which they are resettled. Research shows that after eight years in a new country, refugees will have paid more in taxes than they received in assistance. This means they help the country be strong and powerful.

It is important that people try to help refugees in any way they can. We must also remember their stories. It is important to see that Iraqi refugees and immigrants have created wonderful communities all over the United States. Many own successful stores and businesses, and have made a good life for themselves after their difficult journeys from their homelands.

UN Rights of the Child

Children have the right to choose their own friends and set up their own groups, as long as they are not harmful to others.

Being separated from extended family, such as aunts, uncles, cousins, and grandparents, is difficult for refugees.

Discussion Prompts

1. Who helps refugees adjust to a new country and way of life? Can you name some of the ways in which they are helped?
2. How do refugees help the country in which they are resettled?
3. What are the greatest challenges refugees face when settling in a new country?

Glossary

accountant A person whose job is to take care of a person's or business's money

adjust To get used to something

agency An organization that provides a service

Arab Of or describing a group of people from the Arabian Peninsula who now live mostly in the Middle East and northern Africa

asylum Protection given to refugees by a country

cultures The shared beliefs, values, customs, traditions, arts, and ways of life of groups of people

extremist Having a strong belief in something, often political

immigrants People who leave one country to live in another

internally displaced persons (IDPs) People who are forced from their homes during a conflict but remain in the country

Islamic State in Iraq and the Levant Also called ISIL, ISIS, or Islamic State; a group of extremist Muslims who believe that people who do not share their beliefs are enemies

mosque A Muslim place of worship

racism The belief that some races of people are not equal to others

refugee A person who flees from his or her own country to another due to unsafe conditions

registered Officially recorded

resettled Settled in a new or different place

responsibility The duty to deal with something

rights Privileges and freedoms protected by law

screenings Checks to make sure someone is suitable

taxes An amount of money paid to a government for services, such as education

temporary For a limited time

terrorism The use of violence to force people to accept a point of view

United Nations High Commissioner for Refugees (UNHCR) A program that protects and supports refugees everywhere

Learning More

Books

Kuntz, Doug, and Amy Shrodes. *Lost and Found Cat: The True Story of Kunkush's Incredible Journey.* Crown Books for Young Readers, 2017.

Pipe, Jim. *Hoping for Peace in Iraq* (Peace Pen Pals).
Gareth Stevens, 2013.

Sanna, Francesca. *The Journey.* Flying Eye Books, 2016.

Websites

https://htekidsnews.com/iraq-war-over
Find out all about the ending of the Iraq War.

www.unicef.org/rightsite/files/uncrcchilldfriendlylanguage.pdf
Explore the United Nations Convention on the Rights of the Child.

www.unicef.org/infobycountry/iraq_92964.html
Iraqi children offer insight into their experiences as refugees.

Films

In My Mother's Arms
A documentary about Iraqi children who have lost their parents in Baghdad, Iraq. Suitable for ages 10 and up.

The Breadwinner
A film about a young girl living in Kabul, Afghanistan, who must dress as a boy to support her family. Suitable for ages eight and up.

Index

About the Author

Ellen Rodger is a descendant of refugees who fled persecution
and famine. She has written and edited many books for children
and adults on subjects as varied as potatoes, how government
works, social justice, war, soccer, and lice and fleas.